LAS VEGAS RAIDERS

by Charlie Beattie

Abdo & Daughters
MIDDLE GRADE NONFICTION

An imprint of Abdo Publishing
abdobooks.com

Cover Photos: Rich Storry/Getty Images Sport/Getty Images (Brock Bowers); Ron Kuntz Collection/Diamond Images/Getty Images (Gene Upshaw)
Interior Photos: Chris Unger/Getty Images Sport/Getty Images, 4–5; Brian Rothmuller/Icon Sportswire/Getty Images, 6; Ellen Schmidt/AP Images, 7; Ethan Miller/Getty Images Sport/Getty Images, 8–9, 10, 56, 57; Steve Marcus/Getty Images Sport/Getty Images, 11; Abdo Publishing, 12–13, 58; Ron Riesterer/AP Images, 14–15; Focus on Sport/Getty Images Sport/Getty Images, 16, 21, 38 (top), 38 (bottom), 39, 60 (bottom left), 60 (bottom middle), 60 (bottom right); Bob Campbell/San Francisco Chronicle/AP Images, 17, 18; Robert Klein/AP Images, 19, 61 (top left); Peter Read Miller/AP Images, 20 (top); Charles Aqua Viva/Getty Images Sport/Getty Images, 20 (bottom); Focus on Sport/Getty Images, 22, 24–25, 26, 27 (bottom), 30, 32 (top), 34–35, 36, 60 (top); AP Images, 23, 27 (top), 37; Harry Cabluck/AP Images, 28; Michael Zagaris/Getty Images Sport/Getty Images, 29; George Gojkovich/Getty Images Sport/Getty Images, 31; Tony Tomsic/AP Images, 32 (bottom); Dennis Desprois/Getty Images Sport/Getty Images, 33; Bettmann/Getty Images, 40, 61 (bottom left); Mike Powell/Allsport/Getty Images, 41; Ron Vesely/Getty Images Sport Classic/Getty Images, 43; Al Messerschmidt Archive/AP Images, 44; Paul Sakuma/AP Images, 45; Sporting News/Getty Images, 46–47; Jed Jacobsohn/Getty Images, 48 (top), 63; Timothy A. Clary/AFP/Getty Images, 48 (bottom), 61 (bottom right); Marcio Jose Sanchez/AP Images, 49; Dino Vournas/AP Images, 50; Bob Levey/Getty Images Sport/Getty Images, 51; Thearon W. Henderson/Getty Images Sport/Getty Images, 52; Ezra Shaw/Getty Images Sport/Getty Images, 53; Daniel Shirey/Getty Images Sport/Getty Images, 55, 61 (top right); Megan Briggs/Getty Images Sport/Getty Images, 59

Editor: Rebecca Higgins
Series Designer: Laura Graphenteen
Production Designer: Katharine Hale

Library of Congress Control Number: 2024948506

Publisher's Cataloging-in-Publication Data

Names: Beattie, Charlie, author.
Title: Las Vegas Raiders / by Charlie Beattie
Description: Minneapolis, Minnesota: Abdo Publishing, 2026 | Series: Inside the NFL | Includes online resources and index.
Identifiers: ISBN 9781098296780 (lib. bdg.) | ISBN 9798384919308 (ebook)
Subjects: LCSH: Las Vegas Raiders (Football team)--Juvenile literature. | National Football League--Juvenile literature. | Football teams--Juvenile literature. | American football--Juvenile literature.
Classification: DDC 796.33264--dc23

CONTENTS

The Las Vegas Raiders entered the final day of the 2021 season hoping to reach the playoffs for the first time since moving from Oakland.

THE FINAL KICK

The final day of the **2021 National Football League (NFL)** season was filled with drama. Five American Football Conference (AFC) teams came in still battling for two playoff spots. The Baltimore Ravens, Indianapolis Colts, Las Vegas Raiders, Los Angeles Chargers, and Pittsburgh Steelers would have to give everything on the field. They also had to hope other results broke their way.

The Colts faltered, losing 26–11 to the Jacksonville Jaguars. The Steelers beat the Ravens 16–13 on a late field goal. The loss eliminated Baltimore, while the Steelers stayed alive.

Everything came down to the final game of the season. The Raiders hosted the Chargers at Allegiant Stadium in a Sunday night matchup. In front of more than 62,000 screaming fans and a national television audience, the two teams put on an incredible show.

AN EVENTFUL SEASON

The Raiders had a trying 2021 season. But it was nothing new to the franchise. Despite their simple silver-and-black uniforms, the Raiders have been one of the most colorful professional football franchises for more than 60 years.

Las Vegas was the team's third home. The Raiders had spent the previous six decades in California, bouncing between Oakland and Los Angeles. Now in their second year in Nevada, the Raiders had opened the season with Jon Gruden as head coach. The longtime NFL boss had returned to the Raiders in 2018 after 16 years away from the team. He had Las Vegas off to a 3–2 start in 2021. Then, a huge scandal rocked Gruden, the Raiders, and the NFL. A series of emails were released

HISTORIC ANNOUNCEMENT

In June 2021, Raiders defensive end Carl Nassib publicly said that he is gay. While gay men had played in the NFL before, none had shared their sexuality while active in the league. In the past, many athletes worried that coming out would bring harm to themselves and their career. Some players still face discrimination because of their sexuality. But the Raiders and many fans supported Nassib. During the season, he recorded 21 tackles, 1 1/2 sacks, and one forced fumble in a backup role.

Raiders center Andre James prepares for the critical final game of the 2021 season.

in which Gruden had used offensive language. The Raiders fired him.

That was just the start of the team's controversies. Six days apart in November, wide receiver Henry Ruggs and cornerback Damon Arnette were cut for conduct off the field. The Raiders selected both players in the first round of the 2020 draft. Now, they were also off the team.

A THRILLING FINISH

Despite these issues, the Raiders kept winning. As the Chargers and Raiders kicked off on the season's final day, both teams held a 9-7 record. The winner would make the playoffs, and the loser would be out. In the unlikely event the teams tied, both would make the postseason.

The Raiders led 29-14 in the fourth quarter before Chargers quarterback Justin Herbert threw two late touchdown passes to tie the game, which headed into overtime. Suddenly, the unusual

Raiders defensive backs Casey Heyward Jr., *left*, and Brandon Facyson salute the crowd after the Raiders' 35–32 overtime victory clinched a spot in the 2021 NFL playoffs.

playoff scenario was possible. The teams could wait out the clock, play to a tie, and both clinch their spots in the playoffs. The Steelers would miss out. But the Raiders wanted a win. The team had long lived by the motto of its former owner Al Davis. One of Davis's most famous sayings was "Just win, baby." During the 2021 season, the Raiders had won four games on the final play. Now they set out to do it again.

> **"JUST WIN, BABY."**
>
> —AL DAVIS

Las Vegas got the ball first and drove it toward the end zone. Kicker Daniel Carlson sent the ball

40 yards for a field goal. For most of the NFL's history, that would have won the game. But the league had changed its overtime rules in 2010. Because the Raiders hadn't scored a touchdown, Los Angeles had a chance to score. With 4:35 left, Chargers kicker Dustin Hopkins tied the game again with a 41-yard kick.

The next team to score would win. Once again, the Raiders could have played it safe. Instead, they were aggressive. Quarterback Derek Carr completed three passes. Running back Josh Jacobs racked up big yards. Only 38 seconds remained.

Raiders kicker Daniel Carlson (2) tied a career high with five made field goals against the Chargers.

Facing third-and-four from the Chargers' 39, Jacobs weaved for a 10-yard pickup. Suddenly, the Raiders were in range to win the game and send the Chargers home for the winter.

The Raiders let the clock run down to two seconds before calling a timeout. Out came Carlson for his fifth field-goal attempt of the game. The 26-year-old stepped up and drilled a 47-yard kick to win the game.

It was an incredible finish for the Raiders. The team had already created some of the NFL's most thrilling moments. The final day of the 2021 regular season was another chapter in the history of one of football's most storied teams.

Running back Josh Jacobs's 132 rushing yards and touchdown helped the Raiders build up an early lead against the Chargers.

NFL TEAMS MAP

NFC

NFC EAST

 DALLAS COWBOYS

 NEW YORK GIANTS

 PHILADELPHIA EAGLES

 WASHINGTON COMMANDERS

NFC WEST

 ARIZONA CARDINALS

 LOS ANGELES RAMS

 SAN FRANCISCO 49ERS

 SEATTLE SEAHAWKS

NFC NORTH

 CHICAGO BEARS

 DETROIT LIONS

 GREEN BAY PACKERS

 MINNESOTA VIKINGS

NFC SOUTH

 ATLANTA FALCONS

 CAROLINA PANTHERS

 NEW ORLEANS SAINTS

 TAMPA BAY BUCCANEERS

AFC

AFC EAST
BUFFALO BILLS
MIAMI DOLPHINS
NEW ENGLAND PATRIOTS
NEW YORK JETS

AFC WEST
DENVER BRONCOS
KANSAS CITY CHIEFS
LAS VEGAS RAIDERS
LOS ANGELES CHARGERS

AFC NORTH
BALTIMORE RAVENS
CINCINNATI BENGALS
CLEVELAND BROWNS
PITTSBURGH STEELERS

AFC SOUTH
HOUSTON TEXANS
INDIANAPOLIS COLTS
JACKSONVILLE JAGUARS
TENNESSEE TITANS

Eddie Erdelatz, *center*, was the Oakland Raiders' first head coach in 1960.

CHAPTER 2

A COMMITMENT TO EXCELLENCE

IN THE LATE 1950S, A GROUP OF ASPIRING FOOTBALL TEAM OWNERS got together to form a rival league to the NFL. The new league, which would begin in 1960, was named the American Football League (AFL). The AFL included eight teams. They would play in Boston, Buffalo, Dallas, Denver, Houston, Los Angeles, Minneapolis, and New York.

At the last minute, the Minneapolis owners decided to join the NFL instead. The AFL had already held its draft, and now it was down one team. The league awarded a replacement franchise to Oakland, California.

The new team was established in January 1960. With the season just nine months away, a roster had to be assembled. The Oakland franchise was supposed to inherit the players drafted by Minnesota, but after the original team backed out, many of those players signed with other clubs. Oakland had the opportunity to choose players from other AFL teams. The team, now called the Raiders, had 27 rookies among its 42 players in 1960.

A lack of experience was just one problem for the Raiders. They also

Quarterback Tom Flores was a member of the original Raiders team in 1960. He led Oakland with 12 touchdown passes that season.

didn't have a permanent stadium. Instead, the team played its first two seasons in neighboring San Francisco. They first played in Kezar Stadium, then later Candlestick Park. Since San Francisco was home to the NFL's 49ers, not many fans showed up to watch the Raiders. The team's 8–20 record for the first two years didn't help them draw crowds.

The Raiders moved to Oakland in 1962 but played in a small stadium called Frank Youell Field. It held only

NEEDING A NAME

Raiders was not the first choice for the name of Oakland's football team. The team held a naming contest, and one fan suggested *Señores*, Spanish for "gentlemen." This name won, though the team's owners spelled it as Senors. However, there was soon a backlash. Fans and local officials disliked the choice. The team finally selected another name from the contest, Raiders.

The Raiders often played in front of small crowds in their early seasons, before the team found a permanent home.

20,000 fans, though that season's 1–13 Raiders rarely brought that many through the turnstiles.

AL ARRIVES

Needing a change, F. Wayne Valley hired Al Davis as general manager and head coach in 1963. The new boss would be able to put together a roster and coach it on the field. Davis had been an assistant coach with the San Diego Chargers. At 33 years old, Davis became pro football's youngest coach. But he already had a reputation. One of the reasons Valley hired the coach was because he kept hearing that people hated Davis. Many said that Davis only cared about winning, and Valley assumed that must mean Davis was doing something right.

Raiders linebacker Bob Dougherty (44) makes a hit in a 1961 game against the San Diego Chargers.

Davis immediately got to work. He traded the black-and-gold uniforms the team wore for its first three years for black and silver. Soon, the Raiders' color combination and pirate logo were among the most recognizable in sports.

The coach also cut struggling players and negotiated to get star athletes. The Buffalo Bills tried to sign Art Powell, the elite New York Titans receiver, before the 1963 season. Davis accused the team of negotiating with Powell before the 1962 season ended, which broke a rule called tampering. The Bills backed out, and Davis signed Powell. Powell led the AFL with 16 touchdowns during the 1963 season.

Many of those catches came on deep passes. Davis preferred a vertical offense with his quarterbacks throwing long passes. Picking up many yards in one play excited fans.

Davis proved to be nearly as good a coach as he was a general manager. In his first year, Davis's team improved to 10–4. The huge turnaround wasn't enough to reach the AFL championship. But it was an early demonstration of what Davis called a "commitment to excellence." This slogan became part of the Raiders' identity.

Davis also insisted that the team play hard. The team's game-day schedule always included the phrase, "We go to war!" A former soldier, Davis loved the idea of his team against the world.

THE SUPER BOWL

In 1966, Davis left the Raiders to become the commissioner of the AFL. He immediately started fighting with the NFL, trying to persuade star players to sign with AFL teams. The plan worked and several NFL stars joined. However, unbeknownst to Davis, AFL owners were talking with NFL commissioner Pete Rozelle about combining the leagues.

The merger negotiations were completed after two months. Davis was furious and resigned. He didn't like the deal. He also felt that Rozelle got too much credit for it. Davis thought that his player war with the NFL was a driving force for

Al Davis, *right*, was named the AFL's Coach of the Year in 1963.

Jim Otto, *center*, anchored the Raiders offensive line from 1960 to 1974.

the change. In 1966, he returned to the Raiders. He became the team's general manager and partial owner.

The Raiders' new head coach was one of Davis's former assistants, John Rauch. He inherited a strong roster. Running back Clem Daniels was a dual threat as a runner and a receiver. Center Jim Otto anchored a tough offensive line. Gus Otto, who was not related to Jim, was a star linebacker. The Raiders had a chance to compete for the AFL title that year. If they won, they would play in a new championship game against the top NFL team at the end of the season. This game was called the AFL-NFL World Championship Game. Soon it would become known as the Super Bowl.

The Raiders finished 8-5-1 in 1966, behind the Kansas

Daryle Lamonica, known as "the Mad Bomber," set a Raiders record with 34 touchdown passes in 1969.

City Chiefs in the AFL's Western Division. Kansas City went to the championship game. The AFL was still fighting for respect from the NFL. Most football observers still considered the older league to be much better. They seemed to be proved right after the Green Bay Packers demolished Kansas City 35–10 in Super Bowl I.

The Raiders started looking for ways to improve. Davis brought in a new quarterback. Daryle Lamonica had spent the previous four years as a backup with the Bills. But the strong-armed passer was perfect for the Raiders' deep game. Behind an offensive line featuring future Hall of Famer Gene Upshaw next to Jim Otto, "the Mad Bomber" Lamonica threw for an AFL-best 30 touchdowns in 1967. After the season, he was named the AFL's Player of the Year. Many of his passes went to the receiving trio of Bill Miller, Fred Biletnikoff, and tight end Billy Cannon. The Raiders finished 13–1, and they earned a spot in Super Bowl II against the Packers.

The Raiders' offense averaged 33.4 points per game during the season. During Super Bowl II, the Packers' stout defense kept shutting down Lamonica. Though he threw two touchdown passes, Lamonica

Lamonica hands off to running back Hewritt Dixon in Super Bowl II. Dixon led the team with 54 rushing yards in the game.

completed only 15 of his 34 throws. He was also sacked three times and threw an interception that was returned for a touchdown by

Green Bay's Herb Adderley. The Raiders lost 33–14.

A NEW DIRECTION

Though the Raiders lost Super Bowl II, they had shown that they were tough contenders. The next year, Oakland finished 12–2. Lamonica threw for more than 3,000 yards for the second straight season. But the Raiders fell short of the Super Bowl, losing in the AFL championship game. Despite scoring

George Blanda (16) joined the Raiders in 1967 as a backup quarterback and kicker. He left the team in 1976 when the 48-year-old retired as the league's oldest ever player.

twice early in the fourth quarter to take a 23–20 lead over the New York Jets, Oakland fell on a late touchdown pass by New York quarterback Joe Namath.

More trouble was brewing behind the scenes in Oakland. Despite being general manager, Davis still made hands-on coaching decisions. But Rauch liked things done his own way. In the two years they worked together, Rauch and Davis often argued. After the 1968

John Rauch, *right*, won only seven more pro games in two seasons after leaving the Raiders.

season, Rauch was offered a head coaching job in Buffalo. Despite finishing 33-8-1 in three years with Oakland, Rauch couldn't wait to leave.

Suddenly, the stellar Raiders needed a new head coach to lead them. In what would become a theme for the family-like organization, the Raiders again decided to promote an assistant coach. Davis thought the team's linebackers coach, John Madden, was ready for the job. The rest of the football world didn't really know who Madden was. They would soon find out.

John Madden, *right*, was just 32 when he was promoted to head coach in 1969.

SILVER AND BLACK

John Madden dressed casually, often wearing a short-sleeved shirt and sporting flowing red hair. He was a mismatched partner with Al Davis, who had a gelled hairdo and stylish black clothes. However, they worked great together.

The general manager and head coach cared only about winning football games. Many other NFL teams had strict rules about when players went to bed, how they cut their hair, and what clothes they wore. Madden had no time for any of that. "I had three rules," he later said. "They had to be on time. They had to pay attention. And the third thing was to play [hard] when I tell you to."

Madden's players loved him. The Raiders' only complaint was that his practices were tougher than NFL games. But those practices drove the team to the top of the league. The Raiders went

12-1-1 in Madden's first season but once again came up a game short of the Super Bowl.

Oakland soon became one of the NFL's most interesting teams. Davis put together a motley roster of players. Some had been cut because they couldn't follow their team's strict rules. In Oakland, athletes were judged only by their performance on the field.

The Raiders players earned many nicknames. New quarterback Ken Stabler was known as "the Snake" for his slithering scrambles to escape pressure. Linebacker Ted Hendricks's lean 6-foot, 7-inch, 220-pound frame earned him the nickname "the Mad Stork." As the 1970s wore on, defensive backs George Atkinson, Willie Brown, Jack Tatum, and Skip Thomas called themselves "the Soul Patrol." This all-Black secondary was unstoppable.

Ken Stabler

WINNING THE BIG ONE

The 1970s were a tough time to be a great NFL team. In Miami, Don Shula's Dolphins won back-to-back Super Bowls. In Pittsburgh, Chuck Noll's Steelers were rapidly becoming an all-time great NFL dynasty. The Raiders had to get through both in the AFC just

Jack Tatum (32) had 30 interceptions in nine years with the Raiders, and he was known as one of the fiercest hitters in football.

to reach the Super Bowl. That proved a tough mountain to climb. The early 1970s were littered with devastating playoff losses for Oakland.

The worst came in the 1972 divisional round in Pittsburgh. Leading 7–6 with just seconds to play, Oakland needed to stop Pittsburgh to reach the AFC title game. On a desperation fourth-down play from his own 40, Steelers quarterback Terry Bradshaw escaped pressure and heaved a pass downfield. Both Tatum and Steelers fullback Frenchy

Ray Guy became the first punter ever enshrined in the Pro Football Hall of Fame.

Pittsburgh Steelers running back Franco Harris eludes Oakland's Jimmy Warren on his way to the end zone to complete "the Immaculate Reception" in December 1972.

Fuqua jumped for it, and the ball bounced off them back toward the line of scrimmage. Pittsburgh halfback Franco Harris appeared to scoop it just before it hit the ground. He then raced down the sideline for the winning score.

The play became known as "the Immaculate Reception." It is legendary in Pittsburgh. But in Oakland, Madden and his players were convinced it should not have counted. They thought that the ball hit the ground and Harris didn't catch it. In addition, the rules at the time said two receivers from the same team could not touch the ball on the same play. If the ball had hit Fuqua, the play should have been dead once Harris touched it. However, the officials deemed that the ball hit only Tatum and that Harris legally caught it. The Raiders lost the argument and the game, 13–7.

THE SEA OF HANDS

Two years later, in 1974, Oakland was on the other end of a famous playoff finish. Trailing Miami 26–21 late in the divisional playoff game, Stabler drove Oakland down to the Dolphins' 8-yard line with less than 30 seconds left. On first down, the left-handed Stabler rolled out to escape pressure. As Dolphins lineman Vern Den Herder dragged him down, Stabler flipped a pass into the end zone.

Running back Clarence Davis was ready on the other end. However, three Miami defenders were also there. Somehow, Davis ripped the ball away and held on for the winning touchdown. "The Sea of Hands" catch

THE AUTUMN WIND

In 1974, NFL Films put out an Oakland Raiders highlight video. The narration included a poem called "The Autumn Wind" and was set to stirring music. The poem soon became a team battle cry. Its opening verse read: "The Autumn Wind is a pirate. / Blustering in from sea. / With a rollicking song, he sweeps along, / Swaggering boisterously." The poem closed with: "He'll knock you 'round and upside down, / And laugh when he's conquered and won."

Hall of Fame guard Gene Upshaw played for the Raiders from 1967 to 1981, at one point starting 207 consecutive games.

Clarence Davis (28) falls to the turf after pulling in the famous "Sea of Hands" catch against the Miami Dolphins in the 1974 divisional playoffs.

sealed the win. But, the Raiders fell short of the Super Bowl the next week when they lost 24–13 to Pittsburgh.

A NASTY RIVALRY

By 1975, many were convinced that the Raiders were a good team that couldn't win the big game. The defending champion Steelers were their main obstacle. When the teams met again in that season's AFC title game, the rivalry reached a fever pitch.

They played on a cold day in Pittsburgh. Al Davis and Madden believed the Steelers allowed their turf to freeze so it would slow down the Raiders' speedy receivers. They also thought the NFL would never punish the Steelers. Rozelle was still the NFL commissioner, and he and Davis had a long feud. So the Raiders

A pair of hits by Oakland's George Atkinson were at the center of the team's rivalry with the Pittsburgh Steelers in the 1970s.

thought the NFL would do anything to ensure Oakland didn't win a title. Whether or not that was true, the Steelers won 16–10.

In the third quarter, Pittsburgh receiver Lynn Swann ran across the middle of the field. Nicknamed "the Hit Man," Atkinson slammed his forearm into Swann, giving the star pass-catcher a concussion. When the teams met in the 1976 regular-season opener, Atkinson took another shot at Swann, once again knocking him out. After that game, Noll was upset by the hits and suggested that Atkinson should be kicked out of the league. But both of Atkinson's hits were legal at the time.

It wasn't the first time someone had a problem with Oakland. At that point, the Raiders believed it was them versus everyone else. Convinced they would have to dominate opponents to win a title, Oakland set out to do just that. In 1976, the Raiders finished 13–1.

Facing the Steelers in the AFC title game again, Oakland won easily. The 24-7 victory was sweet revenge for years of shortcomings.

ON TOP

The Raiders battled the Minnesota Vikings in Super Bowl XI on January 9, 1977. The two franchises could not have been more different. The Vikings were clean-cut and calm. With a variety of styles and personalities, the Raiders were loose as they took the field at the Rose Bowl in Pasadena, California. The teams' differing styles were clear. The Vikings, who had already lost three Super Bowls in the decade, were nervous. Oakland was more open and played with freedom.

After a scoreless first quarter, Oakland dominated the second. With the Raiders already up 9-0 late in the second quarter, veteran fullback Pete Banaszak scored the first of his two touchdowns. The 1-yard plunge gave the Raiders a 16-0 halftime lead.

Banaszak and veteran cornerback Willie Brown had been on the team in Super Bowl II. With 6:04 left in the game, "Old Man Willie" put the finishing touch on a championship season. Brown picked off Minnesota quarterback Fran Tarkenton at the Oakland 25. He raced 75 yards for a touchdown and a 32–7 lead. The game ended with a 32–14 Oakland win, and the Raiders carried a jubilant Madden off the sunny field. At long last, the beloved coach had won a title for the NFL's rebellious franchise.

Tom Flores joined the Raiders as an assistant in 1972 before becoming the team's head coach in 1979.

JUST WIN, BABY

In January **1979**, John Madden announced he was stepping away after 10 years of leading the Raiders. He was burned out from the grind of coaching and suffering from stomach ulcers. To fill the head coach role, Al Davis promoted another assistant. Tom Flores had been with the Raiders since their early days. He was one of the team's first quarterbacks. Flores played for the Raiders from 1960 to 1966.

Hiring Flores was a groundbreaking move. Flores is of Mexican descent. He became the first head coach of color in the NFL since Fritz Pollard. Pollard, who was Black, led pro teams from 1921 to 1925. Davis had long supported equality in football. During the 1960s, he had canceled exhibition games in cities that refused to house his Black players in local hotels.

Lester Hayes intercepted 39 passes in his career with the Raiders, which tied for the team record.

Flores took over a team that needed reshaping. Many of the veterans of the Madden era were getting close to retirement. After the 1979 season, Ken Stabler was traded to the Houston Oilers for the younger quarterback Dan Pastorini. Reinforcements on defense included tough linebackers Matt Millen and Rod Martin, along with hard-hitting defensive back Lester Hayes.

UNLIKELY HEROES

One of the Raiders' under-the-radar moves was signing backup quarterback Jim Plunkett in 1978. Plunkett had won the 1971 Heisman Trophy as college football's best player. However, he had a rough time in the NFL. Playing on terrible teams for the New

England Patriots and San Francisco 49ers, Plunkett had spent years picking himself up off the turf after hard hits.

With the Raiders, Plunkett could sit behind Pastorini, recover, and play only when needed. But Pastorini was injured early in the 1980 season, so Plunkett took over. He didn't play like a star, throwing 18 touchdowns and 16 interceptions in 13 games. Oakland went 9–4 to finish 13–4 overall. That was good enough for a wild-card berth in the playoffs.

The NFL wild card had started in 1978. Teams that win their division automatically go to the playoffs. Wild-card clubs have the best records in the conference, excluding the teams already in the postseason. But no team had ever advanced to the Super Bowl from a wild-card spot. It took three games to do it, and often those games were on the road. But the Raiders routed Stabler's Oilers 27–7 in the wild-card round. In Cleveland, they beat the Browns 14–12. After holding off the San Diego Chargers 34–27 in the AFC title game, the Raiders were off to New Orleans for Super

Mike Davis's game-sealing interception against the Cleveland Browns was one of the Raiders' key plays during the 1980 playoffs.

Bowl XV against the Philadelphia Eagles.

Oakland was the underdog. However, the Raiders got off to a hot start thanks to a pair of unlikely heroes in Plunkett and Martin. Martin had been a 12th-round draft pick in 1977. On the Eagles' first drive, he intercepted Philadelphia quarterback Ron Jaworski. That set up a short Plunkett touchdown pass to veteran receiver Cliff Branch.

At its own 14-yard line, Oakland set up another drive. On the third play, Plunkett scrambled around from the 20 and lobbed a pass to running back Kenny King along the near sideline. With no defenders in front of him, King raced 80 yards for what was then the longest pass play in Super Bowl history.

The Raiders never looked back. Martin intercepted Jaworski twice more to set another Super Bowl record. Plunkett was named the Most Valuable Player (MVP) after throwing for 261 yards and three scores. The Raiders won 27–10 and were once again on top of the football world.

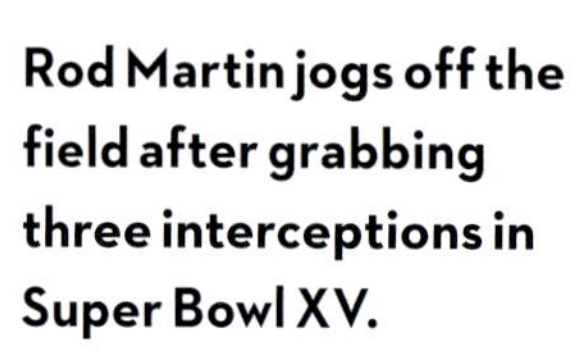

Jim Plunkett rolls out for a pass against the Philadelphia Eagles in Super Bowl XV.

Rod Martin jogs off the field after grabbing three interceptions in Super Bowl XV.

ON THE MOVE

No one knew what would happen when NFL commissioner Pete Rozelle handed the Vince Lombardi Trophy to Davis after the victory over the Eagles. Even though the moment passed drama-free, fans had a right to be concerned. In 1979, Davis had announced his plans to move the Raiders to Los Angeles. When the rest of the league's owners, who had to approve the decision, shot him down, Davis sued the NFL.

Davis eventually won his suit and moved the team in 1982. Despite all the distractions, the Raiders were still excellent on the field. In their second year in Los Angeles, the Raiders won the AFC West with a 12–4 record.

Once again, Plunkett started the year as the backup quarterback. This time, starter Marc Wilson was hurt in the fourth game. The 36-year-old Plunkett stepped in and went 10–3. But the real star of the team was second-year running back Marcus Allen. The 23-year-old rushed for 1,014 yards and nine touchdowns and caught 68 passes.

Los Angeles steamrolled the Pittsburgh Steelers and Seattle Seahawks in the AFC playoffs. That set up a Super Bowl XXVIII

Marcus Allen left the Raiders in 1992 as the team's all-time leading rusher with 8,545 yards.

matchup with
defending champion
Washington. The
Raiders led 14–3
late in the first half
when Los Angeles
linebacker Jack
Squirek intercepted a
deflected pass at the
Washington 5-yard
line and waltzed in for
an easy touchdown.

Late in the third
quarter, Allen gave
the Super Bowl
another signature

Marcus Allen's 74-yard touchdown run against Washington in Super Bowl XVIII was a record until 2006.

moment. The electric running back rushed to the left from the Los
Angeles 26-yard line. His route was blocked, so he cut back. Allen
then spotted a small gap up the middle and sprinted through it.
He outraced several defenders on a Super Bowl–record 74-yard
touchdown run.

The Raiders won 38–9. After the game, Davis was asked how
his team kept winning through all the distractions. Davis's answer
became a defining moment for the Raiders and one of the most
famous quotes in NFL history. "After you have great coaches, you
get great players. You have a great organization. And you tell them
one thing: Just win," Davis said.

The Raiders has heard that phrase before. Davis often told them "Just win, baby." After he mentioned it in that postgame speech, the saying became associated with Davis and the Raiders forever.

SLIPPING

In that same speech, Davis called the 1983 Raiders one of the best teams in history. However, the next two years Los Angeles struggled to get back to the top. The Raiders reached the playoffs but couldn't go any further. The Raiders spent the rest of the decade struggling to field winning teams.

In 1987, Davis made a major impact by drafting former Heisman Trophy winner Bo Jackson. Jackson had been a college track champion and ran like one. He also found success on his college's baseball diamond. Some believe Jackson was the greatest athlete to ever play professional football. A strong athlete, he was 6-foot, 1-inch tall and weighed 227 pounds.

Jackson had been the number one overall pick by

Defensive end Howie Long starred for the Raiders from 1981 to 1993, compiling 91 1/2 sacks.

the Tampa Bay Buccaneers in 1986. However, he refused to sign with the terrible team, and instead joined Major League Baseball's Kansas City Royals. After the Raiders picked him up, Jackson said he would play both sports.

Jackson's signing marked the end for Allen, who had been the Raiders' star back and a popular teammate. But Davis disliked Allen and saw Jackson as his replacement. While both played for Los Angeles for a few years, Allen eventually signed with the Kansas City Chiefs.

Davis also ran through quarterbacks, searching for a big arm that could make the Raiders winners. In 1988, Flores stepped down as head coach. Davis replaced him with Mike Shanahan, but then Davis meddled so much in Shanahan's plans that the coach quit early in the 1989 season. Shanahan ended up with the rival Denver Broncos, setting off a decades-long rivalry between Davis and the coach.

Davis replaced Shanahan with another groundbreaking hire. Art Shell had been a star offensive lineman for the Raiders in the 1970s. He had been the team's offensive line coach since 1983, and Davis promoted him to head coach. That made Shell the first Black head coach of an NFL team since Pollard.

HOMECOMING

Shell led the Raiders to the AFC title game after the 1990 season. But it came at a huge cost. In the divisional playoffs against the Cincinnati Bengals, Jackson suffered what turned out to be a career-ending hip injury. Without him, the Raiders were crushed by the Buffalo Bills, 51–3.

Art Shell talks to an official during a game in 1990.

Bo Jackson (34) was injured on this tackle in the 1990 divisional playoffs against the Cincinnati Bengals. Jackson never played in the NFL again.

Off the field, Davis was once again making big plans. In Los Angeles, the Raiders played in the massive Los Angeles Memorial Coliseum. However, they rarely sold out home games. At the time, the NFL only allowed teams that sold out their stadium to air games on local TV. Davis tried to get a new stadium for the team but failed. Instead, he looked to move the Raiders again.

Oakland had never gotten over losing the team in the early 1980s. So when Davis needed a new home, he found one in the Raiders' original location. The team moved back north to the Bay Area after the 1994 season.

THE BLACK HOLE

When the Raiders moved back to Oakland in 1995, a group of fans wanted to create an intimidating cheering section at the Oakland Coliseum. They bought a block of tickets behind the end zone and dressed all in black. Over time, the cheering section grew, and it soon became known as one of the most famous rooting sections in the NFL.

Head coach Bill Callahan, *center*, and receiver Jerry Rice celebrate the Raiders' 41–24 victory over the Tennessee Titans in the 2002 AFC Championship Game.

ANOTHER NEW HOME

OAKLAND INHERITED A STRUGGLING RAIDERS FRANCHISE. IT TOOK SIX seasons to put together a playoff team. But in 2000, the Raiders started a streak of three consecutive AFC West championships.

The high point came after the 2002 season. Led by MVP quarterback Rich Gannon and star receivers Tim Brown and Jerry Rice, the Raiders went 11–5 before beating the New York Jets and the Tennessee Titans in the playoffs.

That set up an interesting matchup in Super Bowl XXXVII. Jon Gruden had been known as an offensive genius while coaching the Raiders from 1998 through 2001. He was so well regarded, in fact, that the Tampa Bay Buccaneers approached Al Davis about trading for him. In a surprising move, Davis agreed and promoted offensive coordinator Bill Callahan to head coach. Now, in

the Super Bowl, the
Raiders faced their
former coach and the Buccaneers. It was an
awkward matchup. Throughout the season,
the Raiders kept using Gruden's offensive
strategy. Facing a game plan he knew perfectly
in the Super Bowl, Gruden was ready. The Bucs
intercepted Gannon five times, with three of the picks
returned for touchdowns. Gruden's Buccaneers stomped
Oakland 48-21.

Tim Brown retired in 2004 as the Raiders' all-time leader with 1,070 receptions.

SPLASHY MOVES

The next season, the Raiders slumped to a 4-12 record. Davis was
now 74 years old. Many wondered if the game was passing him
by. While other teams were taking advantage of new rules that

Rich Gannon, *left*, watches as Tampa Bay Buccaneers cornerback Dwight Smith returns an interception for a touchdown in Super Bowl XXXVII after the 2002 season.

encouraged short, quick passes, Davis still loved speed and the long ball.

Not one to accept losing, Davis looked for big moves to turn the team around. For the rest of the 2000s, the executive made a series of moves that didn't work out. In 2005, he traded for controversial Minnesota Vikings wide receiver Randy Moss. After two last-place seasons, Moss was gone to the New England Patriots. Between 2004 and 2008, Davis went through five head coaches, including a second stint for Raiders legend Art Shell, who lasted one season. Following Shell's 2006 season, Davis hired 31-year-old Lane Kiffin. He had risen through the college coaching ranks to lead the Tennessee Volunteers.

Kiffin's quarterback was top draft pick JaMarcus Russell. Russell was giant for a quarterback at 6 feet, 6 inches tall and 265 pounds. He possessed a rocket arm that Davis loved. Many expected Russell to be a star. But he performed poorly in practice and even worse in games. In 31 games over three years, Russell went 7–18 and threw only 18 touchdowns against 23 interceptions.

The Raiders picked Sebastian Janikowski (11) in the first round of the 2004 NFL Draft, making him the first kicker to be selected in the opening round.

THE DIVINE INTERCEPTION

On October 8, 2011, Davis died of congestive heart failure. Though his final seasons at the helm of the Raiders had been unsuccessful, no one doubted his outsized influence on the NFL. The brash Davis had built up the Raiders, challenged the leagues in which they played, and always did things his own way.

The day after Davis died, the Raiders were visiting the Houston Texans. Oakland had a 25–20 lead with six seconds left when Houston lined up for a second-and-goal play at the Raiders 5-yard line. Oakland safety Michael Huff intercepted Houston quarterback Matt Schaub to seal the win.

After the game, it was discovered that Oakland, by mistake, had only 10 players on the field for the final snap. Head coach Hue Jackson, in an emotional press conference after the game,

AMY TRASK

Amy Trask started attending Oakland Raiders games as a college student. The team hired her as an intern in its legal department in 1983. Over the course of the next two decades, she rose within the organization. In 1997, Trask was promoted to chief executive, becoming the first female executive in NFL history. Known as a tough negotiator, the popular Trask earned the trust of Al Davis. She was best known for guiding the team through a rough financial patch in the early 2000s. She stayed on as the team's top executive until 2013. Trask went on to become a football analyst.

Michael Huff (24) is mobbed by teammates after making "the Divine Interception" to seal a Raiders win just one day after the death of team owner Al Davis.

said that Davis's spirit had a hand in the play. Fans and sportswriters immediately started calling it "the Divine Interception."

A NEW ERA

The Raiders had always operated as a family. So it was fitting that after Davis's passing, he was succeeded by his son Mark. The younger Davis had a lot of work to do. The Raiders' streak of nine straight seasons out of the playoffs was the longest in franchise history.

It took a few more years to turn things around. In 2015, the Raiders started to show signs of life. Despite finishing 7–9, the team had an exciting young quarterback, Derek Carr. The 24-year-old threw for nearly 4,000 yards. He also threw 32 touchdown passes,

Derek Carr, *left*, and Amari Cooper celebrate a touchdown pass against the San Diego Chargers in 2016.

becoming the first Oakland quarterback to top 30 since Daryle Lamonica tossed a team-record 34 in 1969.

In 2016, Carr threw another 28 touchdown strikes, forming strong connections with receivers Michael Crabtree and Amari Cooper. On defense, third-year defensive end Khalil Mack won Defensive Player of the Year by piling up 11 sacks and three fumble recoveries. Second-year head coach Jack del Rio led the Raiders to a 12–4 record and earned a wild-card berth. It was the team's first playoff appearance in 14 years.

However, by the time the Raiders reached the playoffs, they were missing several key players. Carr had broken his fibula in the second-to-last regular season game. Untested rookie Connor Cook started in the playoffs against Houston. He threw three interceptions and the Raiders lost 27–14.

BEHIND THE SCENES

While the Raiders attempted to get back to their winning ways, Mark Davis was trying to move the team. The Raiders were playing in the aging Oakland Coliseum, which had been built in 1966. However, Oakland didn't want to pay for a new football stadium.

Davis's first plan was to take the franchise back to Los Angeles. At the time, the city had no NFL teams. However, the San Diego Chargers and St. Louis Rams beat Oakland to the move.

Davis wasn't out of options. As his team stumbled to three straight losing records, the owner found a new home. For the first time in franchise history, the Raiders were poised to leave California.

Las Vegas had been a growing sports town in the 2010s. In 2017, the National Hockey League became the first major league

Khalil Mack was the Raiders' top draft pick in 2014. He had 40 1/2 sacks in four years with the team.

to put a team there. The Vegas Golden Knights drew huge crowds while nearly winning the championship in their first season.

A year later, the Women's National Basketball Association moved the San Antonio Silver Stars to become the Las Vegas Aces. They put together a winning season in their second year in the desert.

Davis was poised to deliver the city an even more popular team. With no stadium coming in Oakland, Davis announced the move to Las Vegas in January 2017. Two months later, the NFL owners approved the move by a 31–1 vote.

SILVER AND BLACK SUNDAYS

The Raiders were set to move to their new home in 2020. That left three years for Oakland fans to say a second goodbye to the team. The final home game in California was December 15, 2019, against the Jacksonville Jaguars. After that, the team's last two games were played on the road. One fan dubbed the final home game "Black Sunday," calling it a funeral for the team.

The Raiders jumped out to a 16–3 first-half lead in front of nearly 53,000 black-clad fans. However, the Jaguars rallied to win 20–16 on a touchdown pass with 31 seconds left. After the game, some frustrated fans threw items on the field. But most sat quietly in their seats. Many Raiders players went to thank the costumed and black-clad fans that made up the team's Black Hole cheering section.

The Raiders left the Coliseum for a gleaming brand-new home, Allegiant Stadium in Las Vegas. However, that season was a strange one for the NFL. Because of the COVID-19 pandemic, teams played

A fan holds up a banner at the Raiders' final home game in Oakland on December 15, 2019.

Allegiant Stadium cost $1.9 billion to construct, making it the second-most expensive stadium ever built.

most of that season without crowds. The team's first game in their new home, a 34–24 win over the New Orleans Saints, was played without any fans.

A year later, the cheering crowds returned. On September 14, 2021, 61,756 fans showed up for a Monday night matchup with the Baltimore Ravens. In a thrilling game, Las Vegas rallied three times in the fourth quarter to force overtime. Carr won the game in the extra session on a 31-yard touchdown pass to receiver Zay Jones.

The 33–27 victory was the start of an eventful season that saw a head coach fired and two players booted from the team. Still, the Raiders managed to make the playoffs for just the fifth

Defensive end Maxx Crosby has been one of the Raiders' most consistent players since the team moved to Las Vegas.

RAIDERS
TROPHY CASE

SUPER BOWL CHAMPIONSHIPS: 3

Super Bowl XI – January 9, 1977
Super Bowl XV – January 25, 1981
Super Bowl XVIII – January 22, 1984

AFL CHAMPIONSHIPS: 1

1967

CONFERENCE CHAMPIONSHIPS: 4

1976, 1980, 1983, 2002

DIVISION TITLES: 15

AFL West: 1967, 1968, 1969
AFC West: 1970, 1972, 1973, 1974, 1975, 1976, 1983, 1985, 1990, 2000, 2001, 2002

All stats are through the 2024 season.

Las Vegas tight end Brock Bowers set an NFL rookie record with 112 catches in 2024. He also set a record for rookie tight ends by piling up 1,194 yards.

time in the 2000s. That stay was short. The Cincinnati Bengals knocked the Raiders out 26–19 in the 2021 wild-card round. With that loss, the Raiders' playoff drought approached 20 years. It was a difficult ending to a memorable season. But with a commitment to excellence that had followed the team to three homes over more than 60 years, the Raiders hoped another championship was just around the corner.

TIMELINE

Team owner F. Wayne Valley hires 33-year-old Al Davis as head coach. Davis stays with the Raiders for the next 48 years and becomes the iconic face of the team.

1963

The Raiders lose to the Pittsburgh Steelers in the divisional playoffs on "the Immaculate Reception." It is the most famous of the many playoff disappointments Oakland suffers in the early 1970s.

1972

Under popular head coach John Madden, the Raiders defeat the Minnesota Vikings 32–14 to win their first Super Bowl on January 9.

1977

1960

The Raiders are founded as part of the new eight-team American Football League.

1967

The Raiders finish 13–1 but lose 33–14 to the Green Bay Packers in Super Bowl II on January 14, 1968.

1981

Under head coach Tom Flores, Oakland defeats the Philadelphia Eagles 27–10 in Super Bowl XV on January 25.

Despite the protests of the NFL, Davis successfully sues the league for the right to move the team to Los Angeles.

1982

Art Shell is hired as Los Angeles's head coach, becoming the first Black NFL coach in 67 years.

1989

Davis dies and his son, Mark, replaces him as the team's managing partner.

2011

The Raiders play their final season in Oakland before moving to Las Vegas in the offseason.

2019

1984

Behind a record-setting performance from running back Marcus Allen, the Raiders defeat Washington 38–9 in Super Bowl XVIII on January 22.

1995

After five years of planning, Davis moves the Raiders back to Oakland.

2002

The Raiders win the AFC for the first time since the 1983 season. But they lose Super Bowl XXXVII to the Tampa Bay Buccaneers on January 26, 2003.

2022

Las Vegas defeats the Los Angeles Chargers 35–32 in overtime on the final day of the regular season to reach the playoffs for the first time in its new home.

GLOSSARY

clinch—when a team secures something, such as a win or a playoff berth.

commissioner—the chief executive of a sports league.

coordinator—an assistant coach who is in charge of the offense, defense, or special teams.

draft—a system that allows teams to acquire new players coming into a league.

dynasty—a team that has an extended period of success, usually winning multiple championships in the process.

equality—fairness for all people.

exhibition—a game that doesn't count in the standings.

fibula—a bone in the back of a person's lower leg.

franchise—an entire sports organization.

general manager—an executive who runs a team and is responsible for finding and signing players.

immaculate—something that's perfect, free of flaws.

merger—joining one thing with another to create something new, such as a company, a team, or a league.

motley—made up of many different people.

overtime—an extra period of play when the score is tied after regulation.

postseason—another word for playoffs; the time after the end of the regular season when teams play to determine a champion.

sack—a tackle of the quarterback behind the line of scrimmage before he can pass the ball.

secondary—the defensive players—cornerbacks and safeties—who start the play farthest from the line.

snap—the start of each play, when the center hikes the ball between his legs to a player behind him, usually the quarterback.

underdog—the person or team that is not expected to win.

veteran—someone who has played for many years.